Table of Contents

INTRODUCTION

1. What is the purpose of this book?

2. How can we define faith?

3. Is it possible to please God without fait

CW01501408

4. How can we approach God?

5. Is faith necessary for our salvation?

6. Can we speak of the beauty of faith?

7. What is the relationship between faith and eternal life?

8. Does faith disappear with death?

9. What do we believe in?

10. Is it necessary to deepen our faith?

11. Should we discover and explore faith?

12. What are the fruits of faith?

FIRST PART: THE HEART OF OUR FAITH

I- CHRIST, THE PRINCIPLE OF OUR FAITH

13- Who is the centre of our faith?

14- What is the practical consequence of faith in Christ?

15- What is the foundation of our faith?

16- How to believe in Christ?

II- MARY, MOTHER OF OUR FAITH

17- How is the act of faith structured?

18- Who believed?

19- Can we say that Mary belongs to us?

20- How to receive Mary's capacity?

21- What is the relationship between "the faith of the Church" and "the faith of Mary"?

III- THE HOLY SPIRIT, THE SOUL OF OUR FAITH

22- Who is the soul (heart) of our faith?

23- What is the first grace? And to whom is it given?

24- What is the second grace of the Holy Spirit?

25- How to ask?

SECOND PART: NOURISHING OUR FAITH

26- What are the foods of faith?

I- LISTENING TO THE WORD OF GOD

27- What is the act of faith proper to listening to the Word?

28- What is the Word of Christ?

29- How to listen to the Word?

30- How to put the Word into practice?

31- What is the relationship between living faith and charity?

32- What is the relationship between faith and service?

33- What does it mean to be "moved by the Word"?

34- How does Christ speak to us and guide us?

Igniting the Fire of Our Faith

100 Q&A to Ignite Our Faith

Jean Khoury

www.schoolofmary.org

II. RECEIVING CHRIST AND THE HOLY SPIRIT IN THE PRAYER OF THE HEART

35- What is the act of faith involved in the "immersion in Christ"?

36- Why does Christ give us His Body?

37- What is the relationship between "receiving Communion" and the "Prayer of the Heart"?

38- What is the purifying action of the Prayer of the Heart?

39- Why does Christ invite us to "dwell in Him"?

40- What does it mean to give oneself to Him?

41- What does it mean to "live under the influence of the Holy Spirit"?

42- What does it mean to be guided by the Lord Jesus?

III- LEARNING TO MAKE AN ACT OF FAITH

43- What is an "act of faith"? and what is its usefulness?

44- What is the relationship between the act of faith and the acts of hope and charity?

45- What is the relationship between the three theological acts and the act of "self-surrender to God"?

46- How to make an act of faith?

47- In the act of faith, what part depends on us and what part depends on God?

48- Can we cite a first practical example of the act of faith?

49- What would be a second example of the act of faith?

50- What would be a third example of an act of faith?

51- What does it mean to have "faith capable of moving mountains"?

52- What does it mean to "believe in the prolongation of the Incarnation"?

53- What is the virtue of faith?

71- What is "positive passivity"?

II- JOURNEYING THROUGH THE STAGES OF FAITH

72- What is the path of our Faith?

73- What is the transformation of our being in Christ?

74- What is the goal of the first part of our journey of faith?

75- What is the ultimate goal of our journey of faith?

76- What are the stages of purification and why?

77- What is purification of the senses?

78- What is purification of the emotions?

79- What is purification of the spirit?

80- What is the importance of Guides and Masters for our faith?

III- BELIEVING WITH OUR REASON

81- What is the relationship between reason and faith?

82- What are Rationalism and Fideism?

83- How to achieve the Catholic balance between reason and faith?

84- What does "believing to know" mean?

85- What does "understanding to believe" mean?

IV- PRAYING THE CREED

86- What is the Creed?

87- What are the articles of the Creed?

88- What is the relationship between the Creed and our spiritual life?

—

V- WALKING THE EXTRA MILE

89- Is it necessary to surpass ourselves?

90- How to delve deeper into our faith?

91- What is the Transfiguration? and What is its role in our faith?

92- What is Faith in St. John?

93- What is the role of the Cross in our Faith?

94- What does "blessed are those who have not seen and yet have believed" mean?

95- What does it mean to witness the Divinity of Christ?

96- What does it mean to "confess the Mercy of Christ"?

97- What should our attitude towards Truth be?

CONCLUSION

I- COMMIT TO RENEWING YOUR FAITH

98- Whose responsibility is it to renew faith?

99- What is the importance of faith in everyday life?

II- GOD THE FATHER, END OF OUR FAITH

100- Who is the origin and end of our Faith?

Introduction

1. What is the purpose of this book?

Pope Benedict XVI has called for the Year of Faith (October 11, 2012 - November 24, 2013). Taking advantage of this occasion, this book was proposed to help the faithful renew their Faith. This book will not focus on the truths of faith but rather on how to believe and grow in faith. In a word, what will concern us is not the objective and theoretical side of the truths of faith but the practical side of what happens in the believer: how one comes to make an act of faith and how the Seed of faith grows and reaches its fullness. It goes without saying that the objective side of faith is always needed and is taken for granted as one can find it, for instance, in the *Catechism of the Catholic Church*.

2. How can we define faith?

Among many, we present four possible and complementary definitions:

a) Faith is the assent of the intellect and will to what the Lord reveals to us through Christ and the Church (see Vatican I, *Dei Filius*, Chap. III).

b) Faith is the free and total surrender of our being to God who reveals Himself to us (see Vatican II, *Dei Verbum* 5).

c) Faith is the opening of the heart to receive the Holy Spirit (see John Paul II, *Dominum et vivificantem*, 51).

d) Faith is the eyes of the soul that allow us to see, by the supernatural light of grace, what the eyes of the body and intellect cannot see. It is to see as God sees.

3. Is it possible to please God without faith?

The Word of God says that "*without faith, it is impossible to please God*" (*Hebrews* 11:6). And in Sacred Scripture, the Lord says to each of us: "*I will betroth you in faith*" (*Hosea* 2:22 (20)). Faith is our treasure; it is what we ask of the Church in Baptism, and it is for dying for it that we are ready ourselves (Martyrdom is the voluntary and deliberate acceptance of death by a person out of love for God and fidelity to their faith in Jesus Christ). Faith is our light, our guide, our way of seeing the world, ourselves, and God: it is what allows us to approach God in a manner worthy of His Height and Holiness.

4. How can we approach God?

There are no means to approach God other than by faith. Sacred Scripture says: "*No one comes to God unless they believe that He exists*" (*Hebrews.* 11:6). By making an act of faith, that is, by opening our being to God, not only do we approach Him, but we also receive God Himself. The constant and ardent desire of God is to give Himself to us.

5. Is faith necessary for our salvation?

The Catechism of the Catholic Church reminds us of the need to have faith to be saved. "*Believing in Jesus Christ and in Him who sent Him for our salvation is necessary to obtain that salvation (see Mark 16:16; John 3:36; 6:40).* "*Since without faith... it is impossible to please God*" *(Hebrews. 11:6) and to share in the condition of His children, no one is justified without it, and no one, unless* "*he has persevered in it to the end*" *(Matthew 10:22; 24:13), will obtain eternal life*" (*Catechism of the Catholic Church* 161).

6. Can we speak of the beauty of faith?

Receiving the gift of faith and making it grow within us clothes us with the very beauty of Christ. The more we are transformed into Him, the more we are clothed with His Beauty. Faith in Christ is our victory over the passing world: *"Who has overcome the world if not the one who believes that Jesus is the Son of God?"* (1 John 5:5). We live in difficult times where the sin that surrounds us and its ugliness imprint their mark on our minds, our imagination, and our senses. On the contrary, the light of faith contains in itself the beauty of God, it changes our way of seeing, and helps us beautify the world by imprinting God's beauty on everything. It is also through its beauty that faith attracts us and attracts others to Christ.

7. What is the relationship between faith and eternal life?

Faith is the beginning of eternal life within us here on earth because eternal life is to know God and His Son Jesus Christ and to love them, receiving the grace of the Holy Spirit in us (see *John* 17:3.26). From the first step in faith, with the first action of the Holy Spirit, we begin to receive Christ who transforms, step by step, our "old man" into the "new man." This new life within us, the life of God within us, is already Eternal Life, it is already sharing in the very life of God-Trinity. Thus, faith "makes us taste in advance the joy of heaven" (*Compendium* 28; see *Catechism* 163-165).

8. Does faith disappear with death?

Faith is inseparable from hope and charity. An active faith full of charity cannot disappear. Fundamentally, it is the vision and, in this sense, remains for eternal life. The eyes of the soul or the heart develop with the growth of the spiritual life and become more robust. Having at the beginning "doubts" and "darkness," ley are transformed step by step, through the experience of God, into "knowledge" and "vision." This is our faith: Christ, our Light, dwelling in us, transforming us into Him.

9. What do we believe in?

Our faith is the very faith of the Church. It is not a matter of believing in different realities than those the Church believes in. Rather, the "faith of the Church" enters, step by step, and grows within us, to the point that I believe in what the Church believes. My fundamental and initial attitude is to open myself with total trust to everything the Church believes. This is how the Light of faith develops and grows within us. The faith of the Church is found in various "monuments": Sacred Scripture, the Creeds, the Catechisms, the Liturgy, and the teachings of the Popes and Councils. As we say in the Mass: "This is our faith, this is the faith of the Church."

10. Is it necessary to deepen our faith?

Faith is dynamic and not static. It is like a living being within us, that is, "divine life in us." Baptism is the very "small" Seed (*Matthew.* 13:32) that we receive at a particular moment, but we need to care for that seed, water it until it develops. Reading and meditating on the Word of God, the Creed, and the Catechism, praying, and asking for the help of the Holy Spirit, help us deepen our faith. It is deeply erroneous to think that one is born with a specific degree of faith that will not change for the rest of one's life. Also, a faith that does not grow diminishes. Faith is nourished every day by the Word of God and by the Body and Blood of Christ (see the second part of this book, questions no. 26 and 27). Faith is not received passively but in a responsible manner that requires us to care for it attentively.

11. Should we discover and explore faith?

Without a doubt, the eyes of faith open up everything invisible in God, in the world, and in us. The invisible world of faith is immense; it is not a burdensome obligation to explore it - on the contrary, it gives us joy and delight to do so. It is the world of our experience of God, and He has no limits and deserves this exploration.

12. What are the fruits of faith?

- Greater trust in God
- Greater abandonment to God's will
- Greater clarity during our daily round
- Seeing and discerning God in everything and in our brothers
- Greater perception of God's Providence and His extended hand at all times

When faith is moved by charity, it becomes an experience of God where His presence, His love, and His care are perceived. It grows and purifies until it becomes a deep union with God.

First Part: The Heart of Our Faith

I- Christ, the Principle of Our Faith

13- Who is the centre of our faith?

Christ is the centre of our faith. In Him, we find everything because He is "perfect God" and "perfect Man." Christ wanted to save all humanity and all creation. For this reason, we can see everything "in Christ." Believing in the Resurrection of Christ— meaning the fact that He suffered, died, and rose on the third day — is the centre of our faith; without Christ's Resurrection, our faith is in vain, as St. Paul says (1 *Corinthians* 15:14). It is also part of our faith to believe that Jesus Christ of Nazareth, the son of Mary, is also God (see *John* 20:30-31). Believing in Christ and considering Him as the centre of our faith obviously includes faith in God the Father, the Holy Spirit, and all the teachings of the Church.

14- What is the practical consequence of faith in Christ?

Faith in Christ primarily means having a personal relationship with Him and nurturing this relationship every day. God's love for us has a human face and a human heart: we can see and love Him. God, in the person of Christ, first loved us and gave His life for us so that we might have a personal relationship with Christ. At every moment of His life, because He was God, Christ thought uniquely of each one of us and wanted to be "the Way" for each of us. For this reason, the basis and foundation of our Christian faith is to listen to Christ's personal call and respond to it, allowing Christ to enter our lives, change them, and ignite the Fire of His Love in our hearts, generating in them a great passion for the Glory of God. A Christian life without a personal relationship with the risen Christ, renewed daily, is inconceivable.

15- What is the foundation of our faith?

As we mentioned earlier, the Resurrection of Christ is the foundation of our faith. *"If Christ has not been raised, our preaching is useless and so is your faith. We are found to be false witnesses about God"* (1 *Corinthians* 15:14-15). Three times during His life, the Lord announced His death and resurrection (*Matthew* 16:21; 17:22-23; 20:17-19). This announcement forms the centre of His message because, through His Passion, Death, and Resurrection, He accomplishes our salvation, bringing us from darkness to Light, purifying us with His Blood, and uniting us to Him. Therefore, it is important throughout our lives to delve into the Resurrection of the Lord to perceive—and receive year after year—new dimensions in it. It is important to consider that "believing in the Resurrection" is not an easy act; the Apostles themselves clearly warn us, clearly revealing their failure to believe in the Resurrection. We can see this by reading all the passages about the Resurrection in the Gospels, where we will also immediately have the intuition of Mary's role in this. Every day, when the Priest consecrates the bread and wine into the Body and Blood of the Lord, thus celebrating the mystery of the Lord's Death and Resurrection, he says: *"this is the Sacrament of our Faith,"* and also: *"great is the Mystery of Faith."*

16- How to believe in Christ?

First of all, it is important to understand that Christ Himself is like a "path" that extends within Him from His human nature to the depths of His Divinity. The act of faith always rests on something visible to leap towards the invisible. Therefore, we start with "Jesus as man" and enter ever deeper into Him until we reach His Divinity. Every act of faith helps us take a step along this path. Each time obstacles and daily events present themselves in our lives, it constitutes a challenge to make an act of faith in Christ and enter ever deeper into Him. If we seek "knowledge" or "science," we find them in Christ; if we seek "consolation," we find it in Christ. It is a personal decision to seek these things in Christ and not outside of Him. As a consequence of these acts of faith, the Lord reveals new dimensions of Himself to us, increasing our passion for Him. Every step we take with these acts of faith brings us closer to "Union with Christ," which is the primary goal of our lives. We must always dig deeper into the mystery of Christ and never hesitate to prefer Christ (through actions) over anything or anyone else, especially in the simple acts of everyday life.

II- Mary, Mother of Our Faith

17- How is the act of faith structured?

Our faith is divided into two parts: one is "the content of faith" and the second is "the ability to believe." In another sense, our faith is "bipolar." This structure is evident, for example, in the great Parable of the Sower (*Matthew* 13) where we have these two poles: one is "the seed" and the other is "the soil" that is called to receive the seed. Without soil, the seed cannot grow, develop, and produce fruit. We also notice that the emphasis in the parable is on the "soil" and not on the "seed," on the "capacity to receive" the Word of God and not on the "Word" itself. It is not enough to discuss the Dogmas of faith; it is more important to learn to receive them and let them bear fruit in our lives. For this reason, we say that "we believe everything the Church believes," meaning, we all want to believe in the same content of faith. We must work at it and deepen our "way of believing."

18- Who believed?

The Gospel shows us, in at least two places, that the Our Lady is the only person who could "believe in the Word of God." In Luke Chapter 1, we have two annunciations, one that failed (Zechariah's) and one that succeeded (Mary's). When Mary says "yes" to the angel, she says "yes" for herself and for each of us. She says "yes" for Zechariah and Elizabeth, who could not say "yes." For this reason, when Elizabeth meets Mary, she defines her very well by saying: *"Blessed are you who believed that what was spoken to you by the Lord would be fulfilled!"* (*Luke* 1:45). Mary has been "the Good Soil" (*Matthew* 13:8) of the Parable of the Sower, capable of believing in the Word that God gave her and, for this reason, among all the "soils" that we are, Mary is the only one blessed: *"Blessed are you among women, and blessed is the fruit of your womb!"* (*Luke.* 1:42). God wants to give each of us His Mother (*John* 19:27: *"Here is your mother"*), that is, to give us "the capacity to believe," to give us *"a new heart,"* a *"heart of flesh"* (*Ezekiel* 36:26). Mary is the only one who believed in the Resurrection, a tradition confirmed by the Church in its liturgy. Thus, Mary is "the Mother of our faith."

19- Can we say that Mary belongs to us?

By the faith of the Church, we know that before time, and by the merits of Christ, Mary was born immaculate, "the first of the saved" and "the mother of all the saved." The "yes" that Mary pronounced at the Annunciation and throughout the rest of her life contains within itself our "yes." When God, on the Cross, offers us Mary as "mother," He also offers us all the "yeses" she pronounced throughout her life. Therefore, the Lord gives us an "immaculate capacity" to believe in His Word and receive it as and with Mary.

20- How to receive Mary's capacity?

To receive Mary's "capacity to believe," we need to be humble and ask the Lord for it. The Lord then removes our *"heart of stone"* and transforms it into a *"heart of flesh"* (*Ezekiel* 36:26) in the image of Mary's own heart. The work of the Holy Spirit is to make our hearts increasingly resemble Mary's heart, that is, to transform our capacity more and more into "Mary's own capacity." Before receiving Communion, St. Thérèse of the Child Jesus would ask Mary to sit in her heart so that when she received the Body of Christ, it seemed to the Lord as if He were entering and dwelling in Mary.

21- What is the relationship between "the faith of the Church" and "the faith of Mary"?

Pope John Paul II said in his Encyclical on Mary that "Mary's faith" "constantly becomes the faith" of the Church (*Redemptoris Mater* 28). He added in his *Letter to Women* that the Marian profile of the Church precedes the Petrine profile (that is, "of Peter") (*Mulieris Dignitatem*, Note 55). The *Catechism of the Catholic Church* integrated this profound teaching (see *Catechism* 773). Therefore, whenever we say in the Mass "do not look at our sins but at the faith of Your Church," we must remember that the luminous and immaculate source of the Church's faith is Mary's own faith. Mary is the Mother of the Church's faith and of the faith of each faithful.

III- The Holy Spirit, the Soul of Our Faith

22- Who is the soul (heart) of our faith?

The Holy Spirit is the soul of our faith, as He is the one who moves us to make acts of faith, drawing us closer to God and bringing us into direct contact with Him. He is the Wind that blows in the sails of our soul. Therefore, it is important to be open to the Holy Spirit, to ask for Him, to persist in asking for Him, and to follow His inspirations. It is the Holy Spirit who enlightens our mind and elevates it to God, making it function in a supernatural manner. He illuminates the eye of our heart and allows us to contemplate God face to face. It is our sweet duty to unfurl the sails of the boat of our mind and will, opening them to

21

the wind of the Holy Spirit's Action. Whoever lacks faith must ask for the help of the Holy Spirit. The first action of the Holy Spirit is to draw us closer to God and open us to Him: this is faith.

23- What is the first grace? And to whom is it given?

The "first grace" that God gives to all human beings is the ability to ask for the Holy Spirit. Without God, we can do nothing. However, since this grace is given to everyone and at all times, it is our responsibility to use it and not leave it as an unused talent. The Lord says in the Gospel: *"Ask and it will be given to you"* (*Matthew* 7:7) and also *"knock and the door will be opened to you"* (*Matthew* 7:7). It is very easy to ask and very easy to open ourselves to God, and paradoxically, we do not do it. We must be humble and recognize the presence of this "first grace" that the Lord gives us and always use it.

24- What is the second grace of the Holy Spirit?

The "second grace" is the Holy Spirit Himself, whom the Lord Jesus came to give us, the Gift of God. The Lord taught us not to ask for just anything but to ask for the Holy Spirit (see *Luke* 11:13). This grace, unlike the first, is not given unless we ask for it, using our will with the help of the "first grace." Only when God sees our determined request does He give us the Holy Spirit. The expression of our choice is very important in God's eyes.

Without this "second grace," which is the Gift of the Holy Spirit Himself, we cannot give thanks to God, that is, we cannot have faith in Him.

Let us remember that we are called to receive "grace upon grace" (*John* 1:16), so the action of "asking" does not stop because growth in faith does not stop, there are no limits to it.

25- How to ask?

Several times in the Gospel we see the Lord performing miracles only when people had faith in Him, that is, they believed that He could perform that miracle. For example, in His hometown, He did not perform many miracles because people knew Him humanly and did not believe in Him (see *Matthew* 13:58). When one does not have faith or when their faith is weak, they are invited to ask the Lord to increase it; for this reason, the Apostles said to the Lord: *"Increase our faith"* (*Luke* 17:5). Elsewhere the Lord repeats: *"Whoever has will be given more"* (*Mark* 4:25), that is, whoever has faith. One of the best examples for the increase of faith is this prayer: *"I do believe; help me overcome my unbelief!"* (*Mark* 9:24).

One can always ask for the help of the Mother of God by saying: *"Holy Mary, Mother of God, pray for us sinners."*

Let us remember that Padre Pio said that those who feel their spiritual life is empty or lukewarm should make a Novena to the Holy Spirit. Nine days of petitioning using a short prayer to the Holy Spirit. This method is powerful.

Second Part: Nourishing Our Faith

26- What are the foods of faith?

It is essentially within the Mass that God gives us our "daily Bread" every day. Christ is our Bread (see *John* 6:48). This "Bread" is offered to us during the Mass in two forms: "the Word of God" and "the Body and Blood of Christ." Listening to the Word of God is true nourishment. Receiving His Body is also true nourishment. Prayer, or better said "the prayer of the heart," allows us to continue receiving the grace of the last Communion. Faith "is in continuous growth, thanks particularly to listening to the Word of God and to prayer" (*Compendium* 28).

I- Listening to the Word of God

27- What is the act of faith proper to listening to the Word?

When we open our heart, mind, and will to the Word of God, we make an act of faith. Often an act of faith is made upon a Word given by God. This act does not end at the letter of the Word since it goes beyond, to the very content of the Word, that is, God Himself or one of His Mysteries. Therefore, this "opening and receiving the Word of God" (which is an act of faith) makes us receive God Himself. Blessed are those who listen to the Word of God every day and put it into practice because in this way they nourish their faith in a very powerful way. If on one side the mind applies itself to the letter of the Word itself and seeks to understand it, the grace of God elevates the mind and heart and allows them to hear the very Word that issues forth from the mouth of God. Therefore, Sacred Scripture "is the firmness of faith, food, and a source of spiritual life" (*Compendium* 24).

28- What is the Word of Christ?

Christ Himself is in His entire being the very Word of the Father and His Revelation. Christ essentially comes to us through Sacred Scripture because it is God Himself who speaks in it. Every word of Sacred Scripture has been inspired by God to each author of the Bible. Therefore, when Christ speaks to us through Sacred Scripture while we pray, it can be said that it is the very Word of Christ communicated to us.

29- How to listen to the Word?

The art of "listening to the Word" is called "Lectio Divina." "Lectio Divina" is a Latin expression meaning "divine reading" or "spiritual reading," that is, reading Sacred Scripture with the help of the Holy Spirit. "Lectio Divina" is the daily listening and putting into practice of a Word that Christ gives us through the readings of the Mass.

It can also be defined as a form of prayer where one dedicates a daily time to listening to the Lord who comes every day through our conscience, to speak to us through the texts of the day.

Therefore, "listening to the Word" requires that we pause every day, dedicating time to the Lord who wants to speak to us, opening the Bible (preferably the readings of that day's Mass), asking the Lord to tell us what He wants us to do today.

30- How to put the Word into practice?

When we ask the Lord to speak to us and show us what He wants to change in us today, He indicates through the texts of Sacred Scripture His will, and in response, we ask Him to give us His Holy Spirit to help us put this Word into practice. Thus, we do not content ourselves with knowing God's will for today but by His grace we put it into practice. It is very important to learn "the art of listening" (see on Amazon the book: "Lectio Divina at the School of Mary").

31- What is the relationship between living faith and charity?

James in his letter (*James* 2:14-26) reminds us of the importance of not having a dead faith, that is, a faith that only illuminates the mind but does not incarnate in the will, body, and in good works. Living faith is an active faith where mind and will are united under the powerful influence of the Word.

Charity, that is, "loving God and loving our neighbour in Christ," is essentially "putting the Word of God into practice," which is why the Lord reminds us by saying: *"If anyone loves me, he will keep my word"* (*John* 14:23) and elsewhere *"Not everyone who says to me, 'Lord, Lord,' will enter the kingdom of heaven, but only the one who does the will of my Father who is in heaven"* (*Matthew* 7:21). True charity is not about doing "good things" for our neighbour but about doing God's will: *"Many will say to me on that day, 'Lord, Lord, did we not prophesy in your name and in your name drive out demons and in your name perform many miracles?' Then I will tell them plainly, 'I never knew you. Away from me, you evildoers!'"* (*Matthew* 7:22-23).

As we see, living faith and charity are, in a certain way, the same thing.

32- What is the relationship between faith and service?

As we have seen, it is not just about having faith, but about having a "living faith." "Living faith" is "doing God's will" that we discover in His Word. The Word of God is a word of love and salvation; it makes us like Christ, who came "to serve." Therefore, sooner or later, the Word not only transforms us into Christ but also transforms our works into the works of Christ, which are "service." For this reason, the "New Commandment" invites us to love each other as Christ himself did and invites us to do so "in Christ," that is, "transformed in Him and united with Him."

We are not the ones who decide what type of service we should do each day; it is the Lord who indicates it to us. It can be very simple things, hidden from the sight of others. Often, service is simple, discreet, and humble. We let the Lord indicate to us each day the service that pleases Him. As we see, "faith" and "service" are part of the same entity. Without faith, there is no service, and without service, there is no living faith.

33- What does it mean to be "moved by the Word"?

The Word of God is a word that creates and saves. It "creates" the human being and thus knows him fully: there is no aspect of the human being that escapes the Word of God, its Light, and its Virtue. The Word of God "saves" the human being; it knows his wounds, his darkness, and has in itself all the necessary medicine to heal the human being from his sins and his "spiritual death." It can be said that the entire task of the Word is to seek out the human being with compassion and mercy to enlighten, transform, and unite him with God. The purified human being becomes docile to the Word and its influence. *"The Word of God is living and effective, and sharper than any double-edged sword. It penetrates even to dividing soul and spirit, joints and marrow, and is powerful to discern (judge) the thoughts and intentions of the heart"* (*Hebrews* 4:12).
The desire of the Word is to enlighten us, inspire us, guide us in all our actions throughout the day. With "listening to the Word," we learn "docility," and thus our life of faith makes us "beings moved by the Word."

34- How does Christ speak to us and guide us?

The first part of the Mass, that is, the "Liturgy of the Word," is a unique and privileged moment in which Christ Himself is present among us and speaks to us personally through the "Proclamation of the Word." The Mass is the source of our day. It is in the Mass that we receive "the Bread of the Word." It is through the Word that Christ communicates with us each day — a new and unique Word each day — that He guides us, illuminating our minds and strengthening our wills.

Our conscience needs the Light of Christ, which forms it day by day, conforming it to Christ Himself. In the "sanctuary of our conscience," Christ speaks to us with His unique voice of the Good Shepherd. It is in this intimate and effective way that Christ approaches us and is our Teacher and Guide.

Although this means is privileged, we must not forget that Christ also speaks to us through our pastors and does so in a special way during "Confession" and "Spiritual Accompaniment."

The friendship with Christ that develops in our life of faith is a fundamental element that allows us to always be attentive to His voice and guidance.

II. Receiving Christ and the Holy Spirit in the Prayer of the Heart

35- What is the act of faith involved in the "immersion in Christ"?

The act of faith is a theological act, meaning that it directly connects us to God and gives us God Himself. The "prayer of the heart" is fundamentally an act of surrender to God: the human being offers his heart to the Lord, the Lord immediately receives it with love, takes it, and immerses it in Himself, in His Love. In a certain sense, this act is a full act of faith. Offering oneself to the Lord through the hands of Mary is an act that pleases God.

36- Why does Christ give us His Body?

When we receive Communion, the Lord gives us His Body, His Blood, His Soul, His spirit, and His Divinity. His Body purifies, nourishes, and enlivens our body with Divine Life, and His Soul and spirit do the same for our soul and spirit. His Divinity nourishes our spirit. We are also invited to dwell in the Lord and not stray from Him. He is our true Temple. For this reason, the Lord asks us to dwell in Him (see *John* 15:4) and tells us that without Him we can do nothing (see *John* 15:5). The Lord adds that receiving His Body helps and strengthens us to remain in Him: *"Whoever eats my flesh and drinks my blood remains in me and I in him"* (*John* 15:56). To receive Communion is to make an act of faith, that is, to receive Christ Himself into our being.

37- What is the relationship between "receiving Communion" and the "Prayer of the Heart"?

As we have said, receiving communion allows us to receive the Body, Blood, Soul, spirit, and Divinity of Christ. In fact, "receiving Communion" is the greatest act we can do because it allows us to receive God Himself into our hearts. The "Prayer of the Heart" allows us to return to the last Communion we received, to Christ who dwells in our hearts, so as not to leave Him alone. We have an immense wealth in our hearts, and often we do not use it; instead, we live outside of it, preoccupied with creatures. The "Prayer of the Heart" allows us to use this wealth, to continue receiving from Christ all the Divine Life He wants to give us, that is, the Holy Spirit. The "Prayer of the Heart," helping us to remain in Christ, allows Communion to be fully effective in our daily lives. In this sense, the "Prayer of the Heart" is the extension of the last Communion we made.

38- What is the purifying action of the Prayer of the Heart?

During the Prayer of the Heart, the Lord pours His Holy Spirit into us in a more complete and profound way. The action of the Holy Spirit is to form in us the lost likeness by imprinting the very beauty of Christ in us. The first step of this great action is to purify the human being in the depths of his being. "Purify" means "to remove the old forms of the old man," "forms" that have been imprinted on the human being due to his disordered love for creatures, for possessions. "Purify" means "to remove the gods that reign in the human heart" and "to remove their numerous traces that tire and limit this same heart." Sin causes us to be enslaved (see *John* 8:34), creates darkness, disorders, bad habits, and weaknesses. The purification that the Holy Spirit accomplishes in us through Communion and through the Prayer of the Heart":
- frees us from the enslavements of sin,
- illuminates us with the Light of God,
- brings order to our lives, our thoughts, our will, and our desires,
- gives us strength to do God's will and persevere in it.

With the practice of the Prayer of the Heart, it is often noticed that we are freed from sins and/or bad habits. During the "Prayer of the Heart," the Holy Spirit purifies our faith.

39- Why does Christ invite us to "dwell in Him"?

Christ emphasised that we should dwell in Him, as we can see in *John* 15 where He expresses it strongly. "Dwelling in Him" is the very act of the "Prayer of the Heart." This act puts us inside Christ, that is, exposes us to the influence of the Holy Spirit. In a certain sense, the Holy Spirit is like our soul; He animates our soul: our mind and our will, so all our acts have their origin in God. "*A branch cannot bear fruit by itself unless it remains in the vine; neither can you bear fruit unless you remain in me. I am the vine; you are the branches. If you remain in me and I in you, you will bear much fruit; apart from me you can do nothing*" (*John* 15:4-5). The very act of the "Prayer of the Heart" is a great act of faith that allows us to enter and dwell in the Lord Jesus, in His Being filled with the Fire of the Love of the Holy Spirit. The door to His heart is always open for us; His invitation and His immense desire is to bring us into Himself. We have no other destination or dwelling outside of Christ. Indeed, to have a living faith is above all to dwell in Christ and let Him act in us.

40- What does it mean to give oneself to Him?

Giving oneself to Christ means imitating the child-like attitude by going to Him with total trust, unconditionally, throwing ourselves into His Arms, placing our lives in His Hands. The Lord possesses everything created except our heart and our freedom. Every second that passes in our lives is like an open window or an opportunity to express our freedom and choose to love the Lord. "To love," as St. Thérèse of Lisieux says, "is to give everything and to give oneself," meaning: to entrust all our burdens to the Lord and then surrender our whole being to Him. We can choose to love at every moment, that is, we can offer ourselves to the Lord at every moment. Mary, being immaculate, could give herself to the Lord in the most perfect way, saying, "*Behold the handmaid of the Lord*" (Luke 1:38). She did it for herself and for each of us. We ask the Lord to give us the Heart of Mary so that we can completely surrender into His Hands in the most perfect way.

41- What does it mean to "live under the influence of the Holy Spirit"?

St. Paul invites us to be guided by the Holy Spirit (see *Galatians* 5:25 and *Romans* 8:5-17). The Lord says: "*I will give you a new heart and put a new spirit within you. I will remove from you your heart of stone and give you a heart of flesh. I will put My Spirit within you and move you to follow My decrees and be careful to keep My laws*" (*Ezekiel* 36:26-27). "*I will put My law in their minds and write it on their hearts*" (*Jeremiah* 31:33). The fulfilment of the New Covenant with the Lord's Death and Resurrection, His Ascension, and the Coming of the Holy Spirit introduces us to a completely new way of interacting with God: without taking away our freedom, the purifying influence of the Holy Spirit strengthens it and allows us to collaborate with God with our whole being. Thus, the Holy Spirit enlightens our minds and strengthens our wills, allowing us, day by day, to grow in Christ until we reach full Union with Him. Mary is the model and the perfect realisation of the "disciple of Christ." She has always been moved by the Holy Spirit, and this same Spirit shapes our hearts in her image so that we can follow Christ in the most perfect way.

42- What does it mean to be guided by the Lord Jesus?

One cannot separate the Holy Spirit from Jesus Himself. Jesus is "the Messiah," that is, "the Anointed One by the Anointing of the Holy Spirit." The Holy Spirit is "the spirit *of* Jesus," and He is the One who gives Him to us. The Lord Jesus is also our "Way," meaning: He walked for us. We need to place our feet in His footprints, but most importantly, we need to place our hearts in His. We can do this through the "Prayer of the Heart." The "new eyes" of faith grow through listening to the Word of God and receiving the Body and Blood of Christ and dwelling in Him throughout the day. These eyes allow us to see Christ in our hearts, or beside us, in the events of the day, and also in our brothers and sisters. "Seeing Christ" with the eyes of faith and "feeling like Christ" with the heart of faith allows us to be guided by Christ. The "Union with Christ" — mystical union — grows day by day. On this path, we are helped by the light and example of Mary as the "perfect disciple of Christ."

III- Learning to Make an Act of Faith

43- What is an "act of faith"? and what is its usefulness?

The Bible says, "*the righteous shall live by faith*" (*Romans* 1:17; *Habakkuk* 2:4; *Hebrews* 10:38), meaning that the act of faith procures for us the very Life of God. As we mentioned in question 2, "faith is the opening of the heart to receive the Holy Spirit." Each act of faith we make allows us to receive more of God within us. St. John expresses it in his own way: "*these [signs] are written so that you may believe that Jesus is the Christ, the Son of God, and that by believing you may have life in his name*" (John 20:31). Here we see that "the act of faith" is an opening to the divinity of Christ, meaning that "the eye of the body" sees the humanity of Christ but "the eye of faith" goes beyond and deeper into Christ Himself, reaching His divinity. The act of faith rests on the visible (the humanity of Christ) and with the power of the Holy Spirit is capable of reaching the divinity of Christ (which is not visible to the eye of the body). By opening ourselves to the divinity of Christ, we can receive it and receive the Holy Spirit that emanates from Him. As St. John says, "believing" allows us to "receive divine Life within us".

When Mary believes in the words of the angel and says "yes" to God, she receives God Himself, the Second Person of the Holy Trinity. As we see, the act of faith opens us to God, allows us to see beyond what the human eye sees, and communicates God Himself to us. Faith is the primary means to come into contact with God. Without faith, it is impossible to please God (see *Hebrews* 11:6).

44- What is the relationship between the act of faith and the acts of hope and charity?

The three acts—faith, hope, and charity—are "theological" acts, meaning acts that directly connect us to God. What they have in common is "the capacity to relate to God without intermediaries." But it is also difficult to separate these acts from each other. They support one another and are united amongst themselves.

At the beginning of spiritual life, they fulfil different functions:

- "The act of faith" allows us to see with the eyes of God all spiritual realities and even God Himself.

- "The act of hope" sets this faith in motion and allows it to expect something new, namely, God's Promise: the fullness of union with Christ.

- "The act of charity" finally brings about a coming of God within us step by step, day by day, because through it the Holy Spirit moves our will, leading it to act according to the will of God.

As a person grows, these three acts unify, because the faculties that perform them (intellect and will) grow, purify, and unify among themselves. The being of God is simple, says St. Thomas Aquinas, and the more we grow in spiritual life, the more we are transformed into God and the simpler our being becomes. St. Thérèse of Lisieux is an example: at the end of her life, she reached this simplicity, expressing the three theological acts in a very simple yet profound way—she spoke of "trust" and "abandonment" in God.

45- What is the relationship between the three theological acts and the act of "self-surrender to God"?

As we have seen, the three theological acts unify as we grow, because our being transforms into the simplicity of God's being. One could almost say that the three theological acts become a single unified act—certainly moved by charity—which seems to be a "total surrender of our being to God." It should not be surprising, because the transformation of our being into God continually places us increasingly in God, and any "theological act" we perform becomes a "surrender of our being in the Fire of God's love."

This does not create confusion but underscores the transformation and unification of the three theological acts.

46- How to make an act of faith?

As we said earlier, speaking of the help of the Holy Spirit, there are two moments in the act of faith (or in any other theological or self-surrendering act): a moment that depends on us where we use the habitual grace given to us, and a moment that depends on God, which consists in God's response to this act. The Gospel expresses this dynamism in a very simple way, saying: "*Ask, and it will be given to you*" (*Matthew* 7:7). Faith is the eyes that want (and ask with all our strength) to see God.

The eyes of the body see the created reality, and the eyes of the heart ask for the grace of God to see beyond the visible, as if through transparency. The visible reality that surrounds us, like a "wall," becomes like stained glass, letting in the Light and Presence of God.

Every human being has within reach the ordinary grace that allows him to ask. One just has to use it without expecting anything more, and ask, open the eyes of the heart, desiring the Holy Spirit that will allow us to see with His own eyes. "*Ask, and it will be given to you*" is a sure promise from the Lord Jesus; it must be experienced, that is, asking with all our strength - the Holy Spirit always comes in response to our expressed desire. Then, the Spirit elevates our mind, that is, our capacity to "see," making it function in a new way, infusing into it His supernatural Light, allowing us to see with His own strength: "*For with you is the fountain of life; in your light do we see light*" (Psalm 36:9).

In the Word of God, the eyes of the body and mind see the letter of the text and understand its meaning, and with the power of the Holy Spirit, the eyes of the heart, the eyes of faith, allow us to encounter the very Word of Jesus.

In any sacrament, the eyes of the body and mind see the material signs (water, oil, bread, wine, words of absolution, etc.), and the eyes of the heart, with the power of the Spirit, come to see, to taste, and to experience the Light of the sacrament's grace itself.

In everyday life as well, the eyes of the body and mind look at and understand the events of the day, but if the eyes of the heart are open, asking, desiring, they come to see with the grace of the Holy Spirit much more (Jesus present at our side and in our brothers and sisters) and come to enjoy the active Presence of God. This allows us, on one hand, to be guided by Jesus Himself and, on the other hand, to love Him more consistently throughout the day.

47- In the act of faith, what part depends on us and what part depends on God?

As we have seen earlier, in the singular act of faith, there are two parts activated by two different graces. The first grace leads to the second, because the first helps us to ask, and the second is the Grace itself that is asked for. We will not tire of saying that the first grace is given to everyone, righteous and sinners, free and prisoners of sin, friends of God and those who doubt. This grace is within reach. We do not need to ask for it. It is the constant help that God gives to our freedom and our will to ask God, to cry out to God, to reach out to Him. The prisoners in their cell, in the depths of darkness, in the midst of doubt have this grace: they can ask for God's help, they can ask for the Holy Spirit and will always receive God's gift because God is good and gives us His Love because He is good, not because we deserve it. The Father in heaven "*makes his sun rise on the evil and on the good, and sends rain on the righteous and on the unrighteous*" (*Matthew* 5:45). The Father does not love only those who love Him, He loves everyone (see *Matthew* 6:46-48).

It depends on us then to open the window of the skylight and dispose ourselves to receive the Light of God and in the end to ask for it insistently.

48- Can we cite a first practical example of the act of faith?

To understand concretely how an act of faith is made, we can take a practical example from everyday life. At work, for example, someone offends us with harsh words or bad gestures. The natural first reaction is to follow the instinctive reflex and almost want to respond to that person with the same violence (or more). But instead of reacting in this irrational manner, we take a moment to realize what is happening and the consequences of our response: responding to evil with evil only increases evil and does not bring about a solution. This reflection helps us to pause and seek a solution. At that moment, just two people are involved. If then we open the eyes of faith, we realise the presence of a Third, Jesus Christ, standing between us. Opening our eyes of faith even wider, we seem to hear, with increasing strength, the words of the Lord inviting us not only to refrain from responding to evil with evil, even from being passive and neutral, but rather, with the help of the Holy Spirit, to let the strength of the Lord pass through our attitude, our words, and our actions. What the Lord inspires us to do at this moment, we can only do with His grace: we will respond with kind words, an effort of reconciliation, a smile, an act of peace, a hug, etc.

Here, indeed, we have performed an act of charity, but as we see, it is based on a prolonged act of faith. Upon closer analysis, we realise that the elements of the act of faith are found in this practical case.
- First, only the eyes of the body and mind are open, perceiving the events and wanting to react with their own light and strength.
- Second, we pause and thus allow the eyes of the heart to open and realise the Presence of the Lord. There are not two people involved but three now.
- The eyes of the heart begin to perceive the Presence of the Lord and start to hear (remember) the words of the Lord in the Gospel. The Light of Christ, the light of His words, His way of thinking step by step enters the mind and heart, lifting them up and

making them function in a new way.

All these steps (which will ultimately lead to the act of charity) are indeed the process of the act of faith.

49- What would be a second example of the act of faith?

A second example of the act of faith can be concretized when we take the Word of God, that is, the Bible, in our hands. The Bible is like Jesus: it has a "body", a "soul", a "spirit", and a "divinity". The Bible walks with us, grows with us, giving us the necessary food for each day. When we contemplate the Lord Jesus, we do not stop only at the level of His body or His soul; on the contrary, we also go beyond to His spirit and His divinity: we do the same with the Bible. We know that there is a literal sense (the body (Christ), exegesis (Bible)) and a moral sense (the soul, biblical theology), but we should not forget the spiritual sense (the spirit and the Divinity). There is a similarity between the various levels of the being of the Lord and the various levels we find in the text of the Bible. They open up before us as a path leading us always deeper until we reach the divinity of the Lord. It is always necessary to try to understand the letter of the text, understand it in its historical and cultural context, understand the intention of the human author of the Bible (St. Matthew, St. Mark, St. Luke, St. John, etc.), his theology, his plan, and his goal, but we must also treat the Word of God for what it is: "Word of God," written by the Hand of the Holy Spirit Himself who inspired the authors of the Bible, every word and only those words. In this process where there is "reading," "exegesis," "biblical theology," and "spiritual listening," we live the whole process of the act of faith. The act of listening begins with the text itself in its simplicity and goes a little further, passing through the search for the meaning of the words and their context. All this is a work of the mind that greatly resembles the humble and simple work of studying any literary text.

But the believing reader does not stop at this level; while respecting this first step, he relies on the grace of God and opens himself to deeper perspectives that touch his "soul." He seeks the theology of the author and the meanings of faith, Revelation, and Morality found in the text. This work already relies on the supernatural Light of faith and needs it.

Now the reader, seeking the very face of the Lord, totally willing to convert, with a humble heart and sincere desire, asks the Lord to speak to him, asks the Lord for a word of salvation, transformation, healing. With greater and more powerful help from the Holy Spirit, the believer begins to enter into the Presence of the Lord and begins to experience the Fire of His love, His call, and the healing Action of the Holy Spirit. Here he experiences the Word of Jesus today, uniquely, as "Fire" and as "Salt."

It is true that by putting into practice the received Word, the believer performs an act of charity by doing the will of the Lord, but all the steps that precede it have been the development of a great and true act of faith.

A similar act of faith can be practised every day with the Word of God. Blessed are all who hear the Word of God in Sacred Scripture and put it into practice; they will see their faith grow in a very powerful way, day after day.

50- What would be a third example of an act of faith?

When the Christian, in the silence of his room, recollects himself, enters into the Presence of the Lord, and offers himself totally to Him, he performs a true act of faith, beginning to see with the eyes of the heart the invisible God. "*But when you pray, go into your room, close the door and pray to your Father who is unseen. Then your Father, who sees what is done in secret, will reward you.*" (*Matthew* 6:6). This description by the Lord in the Gospel of Matthew is also a description of an act of faith and its process. To come into direct contact with the Lord, there are several steps to take:

First, our senses are immersed in external objects under the influence of everything happening around us. They are "windows" open to the external world, or rather "antennas" extended to capture messages from outside and communicate

42

with others. To reach God, who is in the deepest secret of the heart, we must withdraw our senses from the world in which they are immersed. For this reason, the Lord invites us to "enter our room," that is, to leave the "outer room," the world, to enter the "room of the heart" where the Lord dwells. Spiritual authors call this stage "recollecting the senses." For this reason also, the Lord called His people to the desert; in the desert, there is total silence and the absence of any creature and distraction. Thus, the People of God can hear Him.

By entering the heart, in the Presence of God, we must unite with Him. It is by calling Him, asking Him, desiring Him that He offers Himself to us. If we do this "with all our heart," this is equivalent to completely surrendering ourselves to Him. This is the language of love that completes all the steps of faith that precede it. By giving Himself to us, the Lord pours out His Holy Spirit, His spirit of love. Here, faith is "alive," "moved by charity," and achieves its goal in union with the Beloved.

As we can see, to find God, we start where we find ourselves in the world of the senses. What the eyes of the body and the mind see is not God, because God is uncreated, invisible to those eyes. For this reason, we must go beyond the visible and, above all, withdraw from it. Secondly, when the senses are calm, the heart is freer to open up and ask for Him. The "eyes of the heart," "eyes of faith," open and look at the present God, inviting us to throw ourselves into His arms. This entire process, which takes us from the created to the uncreated, from the visible to the invisible, from the eyes of the body and mind to the eyes of the heart, a process that makes us desire God and express it with our petition, is an act of faith, and, as we will see, this act gives us God Himself.

51- What does it mean to have "faith capable of moving mountains"?

We all know this passage from the Gospel where the Lord says to us: "*Truly I tell you, if you have faith like a grain of mustard seed, you can say to this mountain, 'Move from here to there,' and it will* move. *Nothing will be impossible for you."* (*Matthew* 17:20). What does it mean to "move a mountain," and to which "mountain" does the Lord refer? First of all, let us remember the context of these words: it was about an illness and a demon to be exorcised, and Christ's disciples could not do it due to their "little faith." The "mountain" symbolises something very large and very difficult to move. The biggest obstacle to faith is pride and the hardness of the heart. One aspect of pride is thinking that we can do it ourselves without anyone's help. In this way, a person closes itself to the Grace of God and does not ask for it. Pride is the greatest "illness" for a human being, and in this sense, we can reasonably say that it is symbolised by the mountain. The more pride we have, the less faith we have, and vice versa. For this reason, the Lord tells His disciples that they have "little faith" (see *Matthew* 17:20) and invites them to open their hearts to His Grace and set aside the pride that makes them think they can do everything on their own without relying on the Grace of God. Having said that faith the size of a mustard seed is always faith, that is, it is always capable of opening up to God and His Holy Spirit and relying on Him. This small faith is opposed to pride, that is, it has moved the mountain of pride.

52- What does it mean to "believe in the prolongation of the Incarnation"?

Christ's life on earth does not end with His Ascension into heaven. We believe in the Total Christ, Head and Body. If the Head is in Heaven, the Body is here, on earth. But they are inseparable. Christ is with us here on earth: *"And surely I am with you always, to the very end of the age."* (*Matthew* 28:20).

When the Lord forgave the paralytic, Scripture tells us: *"When the crowd saw this, they were filled with awe; and they praised God, who had given such authority to man."* (*Matthew* 9:8). We must know that Jesus wanted to give His "authority" to certain men. Our "belief" means "seeing with the eyes of faith" the Lord Jesus present in these men despite their weakness. This is a true and complete faith in the Incarnation and is a great way to honour the Lord Jesus.

———

When we say in the Creed, "I believe in the Church," it does not mean that we put our faith in men. Never. On the contrary, we put our faith in God who wanted to place His Presence in men. For this reason, we say, "we believe" in the Church and do not "see" the Church. "Believing" here allows us to see deeply what the eyes of the body and mind do not see.

For this reason, St. John of the Cross says that God is *"so much a friend that the governance and treatment of man is [done] also by another man similar to him"* (*Ascent of Mount Carmel*, II,22,9).

The Incarnation extends up to this very day on earth, all the power of Christ is here on earth. We activate our faith in "the prolongation of the Incarnation" to receive greater and more assured graces.

53- What is the virtue of faith?

By definition, "virtue" (any virtue) is a "good habit." "Habit" by definition is "the repetition of acts." If these acts are "good," they will generate a "good habit" which is "virtue"; if they are "bad," they will generate a "bad habit" which is "vice." Therefore, the virtue of faith is the habit of faith that results from the repetition of acts of faith. And, as we can deduce, the more acts of faith we perform, the more the virtue grows until it reaches its fullness.
It can be said that the virtue of faith is like a seed, the smallest seed, and it is invited to grow until it becomes a very large tree (see *Matthew* 13:31-32). The virtue of faith is dynamic, meaning that a person is not born with a set amount of faith that will remain with them for their entire life, but rather the virtue of faith in a human being can grow or diminish depending on whether we nourish it or not.

To understand what the nourishments of faith are, it suffices to see this second part.

IV- Clinging to Mary

54- Why turn to Mary? and how to do it?

Mary is the Mother of our faith. As we have seen in the first part, she believed for herself and for each of us. For these reasons, it is very important in our life of faith to turn to Mary and seek her help. There are no limits to loving Mary and entrusting ourselves completely into her hands. It is important to consecrate daily time to nurture our relationship with Mary. This daily act strengthens our faith and teaches us to imitate Mary and receive her into our hearts. The tradition of the Church offers us various means to occupy this time and strengthen our faith with Mary: the Rosary is the most well-known method, but we can also search and meditate on Mary's person in Sacred Scripture, not only in the New Testament but also in the Old Testament as the Fathers of the Church and Masters of spiritual life did, discovering the various figures of Mary. This allows us to delve more deeply into the New Testament and discover more about Mary's role in our faith because there are several aspects of our faith about Mary present in the New Testament but in an implicit way (with symbols and figures). We can also read various authors who spoke about Mary, not forgetting one of the most important: St. Louis de Montfort. We can add Pope St. John Paul II, St. Maximilian Kolbe, St. Bernard, St. Alphonsus Liguori, and the Second Vatican Council in its document *Lumen Gentium*, Chapter 8.

55- How is our Faith formed in Mary?

Mary's Womb, or rather her Heart, is the very place where the Holy Spirit forms our new being, our new faith. God follows the same logic He used for His Son: the Lord formed His Son in the heart and womb of Mary. The Lord continues to form the mystical body of His Son (which is us) in the same "place" because He wants to see us "conformed to the image of His Son," perfect members of His Body. For this reason, we have to return to this "womb" and stay in it, abandoning our entire being into the hands of Mary, to the Action of the Holy Spirit in Her, and repeating several times during the day this act of abandonment and trust. In the Church, we are fortunate to know the answer to Nicodemus' question: "*How can someone be born when they are old? Surely they cannot enter a second time into their mother's womb to be born!*" (*John* 3:4). We know from St. John that we have to bring Mary into our home, that is, into the home of our heart: "*Then he said to the disciple, 'Here is your mother.' And from that hour the disciple took her into his home.*" (*John* 19:27). It is important to walk with Mary, with "the faith of Mary," that is, "with her eyes," always entering deeper into the mystery of Christ. We have to learn to ask Mary to give us "the eyes of her Heart" so that we can look with love at the Lord, always discovering Him more and loving Him more.

56- How to protect and increase our Faith?

Our vocation as Christians is to receive "*grace upon grace*" (*John* 1:16). The amount of grace that God gives us and wants to give us is enormous, and it is very important not to lose it. One of Mary's roles in our spiritual life is to preserve the graces we receive, preventing us from losing them. Just as Mary did for herself (*Luke* 2:19: "*But Mary treasured up all these things...*"), she continues to do so for us. If we entrust our entire spiritual life and our faith into Mary's Hands, she protects it and does not allow it to be lost, so it is important to renew our act of surrender to Mary frequently. It is also important to increase our faith. One of the strongest ways to do this is to thank God for all the graces He gives us. The more we thank God, recognizing the graces He has given us, the more God fills us with new graces. Mary is the best example of gratitude to God, and we can not only meditate but also live within her song, the Magnificat (*Luke* 1:46-55), making it our own. Life and the journey of faith offer us various trials that are also opportunities to purify and increase our faith. Living these trials and crosses with Mary makes them lighter, sweeter, and more bearable and allows for better results from the Action of the Holy Spirit in us. Through the Cross, Mary always introduces us more deeply into her faith and removes everything unnecessary, teaching us through the Holy Spirit the *"poverty of spirit"* (*Matthew* 5:3), which is the very place of pure Faith.

V- Studying and Deepening One's Faith

57- How to deepen the intelligence of Faith?

It is very important not only to learn to act in Faith but also to deepen the intelligence of our Faith. To believe, we need to support our Faith with the Word of God. Once we have made the act of Faith, God makes us enter into His Word, that is, He communicates to us a new knowledge of that Word. This experience of God's grace allows us to see more clearly the content of Faith, almost as if touching it with our hands. This new knowledge should be considered as a new talent entrusted to our mind to make it work. Therefore, it is important not to abandon our minds to laziness but to activate it in service of those insights that the Lord entrusts to it. This search and deepening will allow subsequent acts of Faith to be done in deeper ways. Thus, not only "Faith" is our responsibility but also "the intelligence of Faith". Besides the "Prayer of the Heart" and "Lectio Divina", there are two means offered to us to deepen our intelligence of Faith: reading and study.

58- What is the role of reading in our life? and What to read?

Reading is a very important activity that, if done well, nourishes our Faith. Reading well requires attention, repeated reading, and sometimes taking notes or simply underlining key words.

Reading widens the horizon of our Faith and urges us to deepen and explore it further. Reading shapes our culture, that is, it shapes our way of seeing the world, human beings, and God, and this "way of seeing" is the means, like new oxygen, that allows us to breathe more easily in this world. Culture also serves as protection against various erroneous views of the world transmitted to us by the media and other means. Maintaining a "culture of Faith" is part of the responsibility towards our own Faith.

To "reading", we can add "meditating" and "praying".

Books we can read to consolidate our Faith include: Sacred Scripture (which holds a privileged place), the Creeds, the Catechism of the Catholic Church, the Compendium of the Catechism, the Compendium of St. Thomas Aquinas, St. John of the Cross (especially Book II of *Ascent of Mount Carmel*), St. Teresa of Avila, St. Thérèse of Lisieux, St. Louis de Montfort, etc.

59- What is the role of study in our life? and What to study?

Studying Theology to provide foundations for our Faith is important. Many laypeople today take advantage of the opportunities offered by the Church to study Theology and obtain degrees in it. This initiative allows us to integrate and make our own the twenty centuries of development of our Faith and reflection on it. Throughout these centuries, the Lord has poured out many graces, and by studying Theology, we do what we can to receive them. This study roots us in the "Faith of the Church" and in the Church's own way of thinking about its Faith. This study puts words on our lips to express what we feel in the depths of our being and opens new horizons before our eyes to explore aspects of Faith that we could not have imagined without the Church's experience.

During study, and under the guidance of Masters in Theology, our experience of Faith and the way of expressing it are unified day by day. With the discernment offered by our guides, we learn to reflect in a just and wise manner. This security offered by this path of growth can also become a calling to serve our brothers and sisters and to expand Faith in Christ.

Today, there are several proposals for studying Theology in the Church. It can be a Bachelor's degree in Theology, or it can also be individual courses in the Bible or other subjects of Theology. There are also various institutes of spirituality in the Church where one can learn Spiritual Theology.

Third Part:

Walking and Growing in Faith

I- Avoiding the obstacles of faith

60- Why do we have doubts and what should we do with them?

It's important to know that our journey of faith often begins with hesitations and doubts. These are normal due to the smallness of faith in the beginning, and paradoxically, if confronted, they strengthen faith. In fact, the presence of doubt is a call to make an act of faith, that is, to open oneself to the invisible Presence of God. God is unchanging; His love for each of us is an immovable sun. If doubt stands between God and us like a cloud, we overcome it by making an act of faith—by opening the eyes of faith and seeing beyond the cloud, knowing that God is present even though we do not see Him with our physical eyes or feelings.

Initially, this act of faith may seem quite difficult and obscure, but at the same time, it is exactly what we must do, and it waters the small seedling of faith. Having made this obscure act of faith, we gain an experience of God. Thus, we see that doubt turns into an "experience of God."

When we cannot even make this act of faith in the midst of darkness, we ask God to help us make this act of faith, we ask for His Holy Spirit. God always responds.

Doubt also urges us to seek "a secure Word" on which to base the act of faith. Doubt invites us to seek explanations of the faith that will help us make the act of faith in a better way.

Ultimately, as we see, doubt becomes something very positive. With the grace of God, doubt becomes a springboard to God.

It is obvious that as we grow in faith, doubts diminish.

61- What is the first obstacle of faith?

As we have seen above, the first obstacle of faith is pride. Pride closes the human being off, preventing him from resorting to the help of God's grace. Pride is thinking that the human being is self-sufficient. Wounds and the hardships of life can sometimes shut the human being in on himself, forcing him to struggle to survive. In such cases, it is important to remember that there comes a time when the human being must humbly lift his head to God and ask for help. It is more reasonable to accept our identity as creatures and turn to the Creator, not holding Him responsible for everything that has happened to us, but rather seeking all the positive in Him.

The act of humility always leads to good, while an act of pride invariably leads to evil.

The act of faith, being the opening of the heart to the Action of God and to God Himself, stands on the opposite side of pride. We ask the humble Mother of God to intercede for us, communicating to us the humility of her heart, teaching us how to turn to God at all times. "Pray for us, holy Mother of God."

62- What is the meaning of "ups and downs" and what to do in each moment?

In spiritual life, following Christ, we realise that we go through "ups and downs." It is not a random phenomenon; each state has its purpose. When we have the impression of "feeling" the Presence of God, we should consider this as a grace that sustains us and gives us moments of rest on the journey, preparing us for the next actions. Conversely, when we have the impression of "feeling" the absence of God—a harsh and sometimes infernal impression—we must remember that this is the moment *par excellence* to make a good act of faith. We must recall the preceding moments when we had the impression of "being in paradise" and "feeling" the Presence of God, to encourage ourselves and make a good act of faith. Without these moments of "emptiness," we would be content to remain in the pleasure we feel, enjoying those feelings. Indeed, all these changes are made intentionally by God, who offers us "milk," as St. Paul says (1 Corinthians 3:2), alternating these moments with weaning moments to urge us to activate our inner "muscles", i.e. the theological acts of Faith, Hope and Love.

The human being who relies on the "feeling" of God's presence or absence is like one who walks "with crutches," while the human being who goes to God "with faith" and grows is the one who uses his own muscles with "divine blood" (the Holy Spirit). Being weak at first, the Lord cannot always impose on us the need to make acts of faith; for this reason, His wisdom chooses to alternate brief moments of rest with moments of "exercise" for growth.

63- Where to seek God?

The spiritual path invites us to leave creatures behind and go towards the Creator. Our heart has been created "by God," "in the image of God," and only God is capable of filling and satisfying it. Many times, we exchange God for other gods. We put these gods on the throne of our heart.

God dwells at the centre of our being, in our heart, while the creatures we transform into gods through our desires are outside our being. If we allow ourselves to be drawn to creatures, we find ourselves outside the home of our heart, suffering from the absence of God and from an ever greater and never satisfied thirst. We do not understand our heart and do not know its true nourishment.

64- What does the love of creatures provoke in us?

There are two ways to love creatures. We either love them "for God" and "because of God," or we love them "as gods," meaning they occupy our entire heart, our entire being, all our search, and all our desires. Love has this property of "transforming the lover into the beloved." In this sense, the love of creatures (which makes gods of them) transforms our heart to resemble them. Thus, our heart diminishes, suffers greatly, and becomes thirstier for true happiness without knowing how to obtain it. Misled, our desires lead us outward where the creatures are, leaving God (who is our supreme good and true happiness) locked up and alone in the depths of our heart.

65- What does temptation consist of?

Living often outside of ourselves with creatures, moved by our idolatrous love for them, humans become easy prey for the Tempter. Instead of looking towards the Lord within, the human turns 180 degrees outward towards creatures. In this case, temptation is much more frequent. When we say in the Our Father, "lead us not into temptation," we are actually saying: "when temptation comes and our gaze turns towards creatures, help us, Lord, with your Grace to turn 180 degrees towards God who is in the depths of our heart."

What is at stake it no fighting against the devil, for it would be an act of pride to pretend to be able to defeat a spirit; and fighting with him reinforces our tendency to be outside with creatures. On the contrary, it's about, with the Grace of God, leaving the devil where he is, turning towards God who is within us, and throwing ourselves into His Arms. This results in consolidating our "windows," which are our senses, and step by step learning to close them. It's not about isolating ourselves from the external world but having God as "our dwelling place," that is, the place where we constantly are when in relationship with creatures and loving them starting from God and for God. Step by step, we thus learn to dwell within our heart with the Lord, experiencing His Presence and Love.

66- What does it mean to believe in "one God"?

Often when we see the strength of temptation, we are tempted to go beyond it, considering the devil as a "god of evil," and life as a struggle between "the god of evil" and "the God of good." This also leads us to fear the devil in a disordered and exaggerated way or to see him everywhere. This worldview is fundamentally

erroneous. In the Creed, we say that "we believe in one God." T
means that there are no other gods, and it also means that the
devil himself (who is only a creature) is subject to God, and all
his actions are as well, and nothing that happens in our life from
the devil occurs without God's direct permission. For this reason,
we must strengthen our faith in the uniqueness of God and fear
only God. The "fear of God," the "Christian fear" of God, is the
fear of a child who does not want to hurt his father with actions
that sadden him. It is not a fear of terror; it is a fear born of filial
love for the Father. Therefore, it is important to look only to God,
seek only Him, and fear no one outside of Him, knowing that His
Providence watches over us all the time to the extent that if a hair
falls from our head, the Lord sees it (see *Matthew* 10:30).

67- What are the temptations against faith?

In our journey of growth, our faith encounters several temptations against it.
The first temptation is pride, as we have seen before.
The second is not believing in everything the Church believes.
Indeed, God placed the "Deposit of Faith" in the Church and
invites us to receive it integrally, to preserve it, and to transmit it
to future generations.
The third temptation is to stray from the Word of God, seeking
other sources to receive Revelation and the daily nourishment of
our faith. Linked to this temptation is the temptation to hear the
Word but not put it into practice.
The fourth temptation is to stay away from the Mass, because the
Mass is the summit and source of our day; everything we need
can be found within the Mass. Linked to this temptation is the
temptation not to do the "Prayer of the Heart." As St. John of the
Cross says: "whoever flees from prayer, flees from all that is
good" (*Sayings of Light*).
The fifth temptation is not to resort to God's Mercy and His
Forgiveness in the Sacrament of Confession.
The sixth temptation is to allow our faith to die, to separate it
from charity towards our neighbour. A faith that forgets the
brother is a faith in serious danger.

The seventh temptation should be the first and the one that encompasses everything. It consists of not accepting the primacy of Mary in the order of faith as "she alone who believed in the Word" and "she who forms the faith of each of us."

68- The synergy between the Holy Spirit and us?

Faith is an act that puts us in direct contact with God. This contact allows the Lord to pour out His Holy Spirit on us. Thus, a relationship is created between "the Holy Spirit (and His Action)" and "our way of responding to the Action of the Holy Spirit." The relationship between both actions must be realised in "harmony," and theologically, this harmony is called "synergy." It is a Greek word composed of two parts: "syn" (in Greek meaning "with") and "energy"; that is, to act together.

The better to understand this harmony and the relationship that exists between the Holy Spirit and us, we can take the example of dancing. Watching two people who dance well gives the impression that they do so effortlessly. Let us examine three examples that will help us to understand correctly the "synergy" between the Action of the Holy Spirit and ours.

69- What is "negative passivity"?

A first possibility of relationship in dance is the "negative passivity" on the part of the "woman." The Holy Spirit is represented by the "man" and we by the "woman." Sometimes it is thought that God, being Almighty, has to do everything in our lives and we do nothing. This is translated in the example of dance when the "woman" thinks she does not have to do anything and that the "man" will do everything, that is, to dance with her, he will move her like a puppet. This case completely cancels out the faculties of the human being, completely removing freewill, commitment, the use of the mind, of the will, of the imagination, etc. It is obvious that this "negative passivity" does not translate the correct synergy that God wants from us.

70- What is "negative activism"?

The second possibility of relationship in dance is the "negative activism" on our part. In this case, we respond actively to the Lord's invitation, but we are the ones who guide the Lord in the dance deciding where to go and what to do. We continue with our preferences, the places where we want to go (looking at where we put our feet), the people with whom we want to deal and "force" the Lord to follow everything we do, we ask Him to help us succeed. In this case, although we are active and sometimes very active, we do not realise that we do not really trust the Lord and have not given our entire lives into His hands and indeed do not consider Him as the true Boss. In this way, we are owners of our faith and do not let ourselves be guided by the Holy Spirit and do not listen to His inspirations. Our faith here has much of the human.

71- What is "positive passivity"?

The third and final possibility of relationship with the Holy Spirit is "positive passivity." In it, we look at the Lord face to face and allow ourselves to be guided in the dance by His arms. That is, we have total confidence in the Lord, knowing that wherever He leads us, we will be safe with Him and that all the paths He proposes to us and guides us on are good. It is true that we let Him guide us, but it is also true that we are attentive to all the signs and impulses that the Lord sends us through His Spirit. In this case, we make an effort, but it is an effort of docility, a humble effort of listening and harmonious correspondence to His will and His promptings, without rigidity. This effort is the most difficult and is the result of a long time of friendship with the Lord in which we have allowed ourselves to be transformed and purified by Him, learning to let Him guide us "where He wants" and "as He wants." Abandoning ourselves to the will of God is the best fulfilment of this effort.

II- Journeying through the stages of Faith

72- What is the path of our Faith?

As we have said before, our faith is like a seed that needs to develop until it becomes a great tree that bears fruit. Between "the first steps," that is, "the seed form," and "the time of maturity," when the tree bears its fruit, we have a path of growth. Over twenty centuries, spiritual Masters have managed to describe this path and its stages to us. Many began to do so by seeing, in a new way, the very path of the people of God when they left Egypt to reach the Promised Land. The various stages of the journey of the people of Israel have been seen by spiritual Masters as a reflection of the stages of growth of human faith until it reaches its fullness (see 1 *Corinthians* 10:1-6).

Other authors have considered Moses' ascent of Mount Sinai also as an example of purification and transformation until reaching the full maturity of faith, that is, the contemplation of the Trinity within the Trinity itself. Still other authors preferred the image of the ladder through which they described the different stages of growth. All have agreed to say what St. Paul has already said in his letters, that is, we must move from "milk" for infants to "solid food" (see 1 *Corinthians* 3:1-2). The life of faith in Christ must grow until it reaches *"the perfect man, to the measure of the full stature of Christ"* (*Ephesians* 4:13).

73- What is the transformation of our being in Christ?

One of the first and most fundamental actions of Christ in us is to purify our faith. Let us remember that He said: *"Blessed are the pure in heart, for they shall see God"* (*Matthew* 5:8). For Christ to live in us and act through us freely, we must be pure. Let us also remember that the great project of the monks was to achieve this purification and all the spiritual Masters have explained to us the various stages of purification of our being in order to be able to see God, that is, to reach Union with Christ.

74- What is the goal of the first part of our journey of faith?

The Masters of spiritual life tell us that, after our purification, our faith allows us to unite more fully with the Lord Jesus Christ. As St. Paul recalls in the letter to the Ephesians, we must reach "*the fullness of Christ,*" "*the fullness of His height.*" St. Paul expresses this stage in another way when he says, "*It is no longer I who live, but Christ who lives in me*" (*Galatians* 2:20). St. Teresa of Avila and St. John of the Cross and other holy Doctors used other words to express this first goal of the journey of our faith: "union with God," "spiritual marriage," "acquisition of the Holy Spirit."

75- What is the ultimate goal of our journey of faith?

Undoubtedly, the final goal of our life on earth is, to be with Christ and in Christ, to imitate His death, that is, to fully realise His New Commandment: "*You must love one another as I have loved you*" (*John* 13:34; 15:12) and also, "*There is no greater love than to lay down one's life for one's friends*" (*John* 15:13). The fullness of Charity is the pinnacle of the development of our faith here below.

"Since Jesus, the Son of God, manifested his love by giving his life for us, no one has greater love than this, to give his life for him and his brothers" (cf. 1 *John* 3:16; *John* 15:13). Well: some Christians, even from the beginning, were called, and will continue to be called, to give this supreme testimony of love to all, especially to the persecutors. Therefore, martyrdom, in which the disciple resembles the Master, who freely accepted death for he salvation of the world and conforms to Him in the outpouring of his blood, is esteemed by the Church as an eminent gift and the supreme test of love. Although it is a gift granted to a few, however, all must be prepared to confess Christ before men and follow Him, by the way of the cross, amidst the persecutions that are never lacking in the Church." (*Second Vatican Council, Lumen Gentium,* 42)

Faith is our greatest treasure, it is the means by which we receive God. It is a great grace to be called to die for it.

76- What are the stages of purification and why?

The stages of purification follow the different parts of our being. We are composed of body (senses, etc.), soul (conscious mind and will, etc), and spirit (supraconscious mind and will, etc.). Generally, the Lord purifies us starting with the lowest and outermost (the body) to the highest and innermost (the spirit).

There are sometimes exceptions in the order of purification, especially when there are certain very serious sins that hinder a person's progress, and also in the case of "invincible ignorance" (like St. Paul who thought he was doing good by persecuting the Church). In these exceptions, the Lord gives stronger and more advanced graces to free the human being from a strong enslavement. But then He returns to proceeding in the normal order.

The Lord begins with the body and the senses because simply the "old man" lives outside himself, immersed in the material world, attracted by it, and often enslaved by various vices. So, the Lord starts from where we are; it is the Lord who descends to make us rise. And the Lord continues taking steps forward by entering further, that is, purifying the soul, etc., until reaching the spirit.

77- What is purification of the senses?

As we were saying, the vast majority of human beings, when they begin the spiritual journey, direct their tendencies and inclinations outward, that is, towards creatures. Through the senses (seeing, feeling, smelling, etc.), the human being reaches the visible world but also runs the risk of becoming attached to what he finds in this world: it can be food, pleasure, money, material goods, human glory, appearances, power, etc.

When this same human being begins his journey with the Lord, the Lord descends to the level of the human being and begins the purification journey of his faith. Speaking the language of the person, the Lord begins by proposing alternatives to these attachments and enslavements. For this reason, the Lord says that we must fast and pray. By fasting "with the Grace of God" and "for the love of Jesus Christ," the human being chooses the Lord over his vices, sins, or attachments, but does so for the love of Christ and with the grace of Christ. Through Prayer and listening to the Word of God, the human being receives the strength of the Holy Spirit and the work of purification that He does in him.

At the end of this stage of purification, the human being experiences a first great liberation where he tests self-possession and the rule of the soul over the body. (see St. Teresa of Avila description of "Union of will" in "Interior Castle" Fifth Mansions.)

78- What is purification of the emotions?

Living this first victory, the human being feels called to learn to love his neighbour with a purer heart. The Lord shows him with the Light of His Spirit how his way of loving his neighbour is low and short-lived, how much there is of human in this love and how much the preferences of the "old man" interfere with the love of neighbour.

The Lord begins to call the human being to let himself be purified and to go out of himself and his preferences and tastes. The Lord shows to our emotions the narrow path of pure love of the Lord, where one loves one's neighbour not "by preferences" or "tastes" but "for the love of the Lord," without making distinctions between people, moments, and ways.

The human being begins to realise the sacrifice he must make to put the Lord above any other relationship, including the most beloved people (parents, children, spouse, etc.). At this level, the demands of the Lord and of faith in Him seem greater and stronger.

After the fire of this purification, the human being finds himself closer and more intimate with the Lord and experiences a much more penetrating faith, victorious over many obstacles.

79- What is purification of the spirit?

After these two great stages, the faith of the human being is already much more solid, more rooted in the Lord, but still lacking the last stage of purification, which is in fact the greatest: it is about purifying the very core of the human being, that is, his "ego."

In this final battle, the toughest one, the fire of the Holy Spirit concentrates on the human being's "ego," the "I," and begins with all the weight of God's Holiness to teach from within, as no one else can do, humility, God's very humility.

Before this purification, the human being resembles the Apostle Peter who tells the Lord that he is ready to give his life for Him (see *John* 13:37). During this purification, the human being experiences his denial of his Lord, just as Peter did, his own radical weakness, his lack of faith in the Resurrection, and the need to turn to Mary to believe and to find the Risen One.

The human being realises how much he owes to Mary and the abyss that separates all human beings from Mary in the sense that she is "the only one who believed." The human being learns to turn to Mary to let the "new creature" and the "new man" be born in him.

While faith grows and purifies, so does the strong desire to see the Lord and His divinity. As the purification ends, the human being receives the grace of a new and strong vision of the Lord marking a new stage that the masters call "spiritual betrothal" (*St. John of the Cross*, *Spiritual Canticle* A,12).

80- What is the importance of Guides and Masters for our faith?

The path of faith is not a solitary journey, but rather a journey within the Church of Christ. The Creed invites us to "believe in the Church," because what is seen of the Church has two possible origins: it is either "from God through His servants" or "from human beings who compose the Church" and who sometimes, when they sin, are not of the Church. For this reason, we have to "believe in the Church," that is, to go beyond and deeper than what is seen, seeking God. If we seek God only within the Church, we will always find Him and in great abundance.

The Lord places Guides and Masters on our path in the persons of friends, priests, monks, and nuns. It is the will and desire of the Lord to speak to us through them. It is a necessity for us to receive the discernment of faith through them. This humble act of faith that recognizes Christ present in His Church has a great price in the eyes of the Lord and is a source of great graces, spiritual progress, and security on the path. This act defeats the devil. Many people who seek to grow in their faith and do not make this act of humility and praise to the Incarnation stray and do not reach the fullness of faith, that is, union with Christ-God.

III- Believing with our Reason

81- What is the relationship between reason and faith?

It is with our mind moved by our will that we make the act of believing. It does not simply cancelling or erasing reason but allowing the supernatural light of God to enter our mind to illuminate it, elevate it, and make it operate in a higher mode. Without the mind, there is no act of faith.

"The natural light of reason" and "the supernatural light of faith" belong to two different orders or levels. But it must be recognised that "the supernatural light of faith" never contradicts the "natural light" of reason. It rather elevates it by adding its strength and height.

We can also compare the relationship between "reason" and "faith" or rather "reason" and "the supernatural light of faith" as "the soil" and a "seed of Light." Without the "soil," the "seed" cannot grow and bear fruit; similarly, without the "seed of light," which is God's gift, reason cannot reach such heights as God and the mysteries of the Christian faith.

82- What are Rationalism and Fideism?

Managing the relationship between "human reason" and its functioning on one side and "the light of faith" and its functioning on the other side is something very delicate that needs balance. Excesses on either side can lead to deviations in functioning, breaking the delicate harmony that should exist.

The first excess we can observe is when reason wants to do everything or almost everything with its natural light alone. This excess is called "rationalism." In this case, the human mind does not leave sufficient space for the light of God, the help of the Holy Spirit, and the entire supernatural world of God and His mysteries that are beyond the reach of natural light. By closing itself to its higher functioning, the human mind remains struggling alone, thinking (with a certain pride and pretension) that it can find answers to everything and reach God Himself without God's help.

The second excess is "fideism." This excess on the other side, that is, on the supernatural side, occurs when the human being forgets to offer to "the Seed of light" the "soil" of his own mind and falls into condemnable laziness. The true supernatural line to follow is then mixed and modified by several falsely "spiritual" elements, which are not necessarily founded in true faith. In that case, it can be said that the person is asking a lot from God and

66

doing little to receive it, offering little space in his mind to receive the seed of light. The seed then cannot take root in the mind. When God speaks to us, giving us His supernatural light, we have to use our entire mind to receive this light and activate it in His service. Remaining only in an "attitude of faith" without "wanting to understand" is like not wanting to take responsibility for the received Seed. The light of God is meant to fertilize our mind and not leave it in unfruitful laziness.

Both extremes do not offer the right relationship for the harmonious development of the seeds of light in the soil of our mind. Creating imbalances abort the seed that does not bear fruit.

83- How to achieve the Catholic balance between reason and faith?

From the previous question, we can deduce that the typical Catholic balance between reason and faith is to give the entire space both to reason as soil to receive the seed of light and to that same Seed. It is not about choosing between reason and faith but uniting both realities in a harmonious, active, interactive and productive relationship for superior fecundity.

Of course, this relationship between reason and supernatural light creates tension, but it is a healthy tension. It also generates greater responsibility on our part: - first, that of treating God as God, that is, understanding that His gifts belong to a completely different level or order and that we need His intervention; - second, that of honouring, with responsibility and commitment, our intellect, pushing it not only to receive the light of God but also to activate it in His service, seeking, with the grace of God, to always understand more fully the truths of faith and serve them with all our strength.

It is obvious that to maintain this balance between reason and supernatural light, one must pray or, as they say today, with a "kneeling" mind so to speak, that is, with the humility of one who asks, who seeks, and who knocks on the door of God Himself.

84- What does "believing to know" mean?

Christian tradition has traced a way for us to walk, that is, manage the relationship between reason and faith, indicating them as two "legs" on which to walk well and grow. The first "leg" is "believing to know," and the second is "understanding to believe."

First of all, we need to "believe to know." To approach God, we need to believe that He is present and that He is speaking to us. We also need to search for His Words and find them in Sacred Scripture. His Words being *"Spirit and Life"* (see *John* 6:63). Having the Word of the Lord before us, we are called to make an act of faith that it is the "Word of God" and that "God uses it to speak to us." In this sense, we open ourselves to the action of the Spirit and of Divine Life found in that Word. The action of the Holy Spirit elevates our mind to help us know that Word in a new way, from within, under the Light of God. If we give space to that Word in our being, in our will, and in our body, putting it into practice, then we will have a new experience of that same Word: we move from a pure "understanding" with the intellect to a full "knowing" involving all our being.

We can conclude by saying that the fact of having believed in the Word, of having asked for the light and strength of the Holy Spirit to put it into practice, has given us a new "knowing".

85- What does "understanding to believe" mean?

The other "leg" that we have to learn to use is "understanding to believe." It is important to know that the two legs work one after the other, which means that there are two actions of "understanding"/ "knowing": one prepares to believe (understanding), and the other explores what has been believed and known. In fact, in order to believe, we must have a minimum of understanding with reason to make an act of faith. The act of faith is based on a Word that the Lord gives us. We have to understand that Word as much as possible with the light of reason and the general light of faith. This understanding is only initial, to make the act of faith.

Once the act of faith has been made, we receive a new supernatural knowledge of the Word we have believed. This knowledge offers our mind, illuminated by the Holy Spirit, a new field for exploration and new understandings.

It is very important to learn to walk well with these two legs and realise that each step we take is equivalent to a climb towards God: our mind at the same time is transformed in Christ and takes new responsibilities towards the light of God and His mysteries and the multiple ways to incarnate them every day.

IV- Praying the Creed

86- What is the Creed?

The Creed is a collection ("symbol") of the major articles of our Christian faith. It contains everything we believe and is therefore considered the fundamental criterion and reference of our faith. In it, the Trinity, the Incarnation, Salvation, the Church, and the Sacraments are revealed.

The Creed is the most precious jewel of our Christian life. It opens several windows to God Himself, His infinity, His intimate life, and His works of salvation. It is transmitted to us during Baptism, and in ancient times, it was not written but given orally to catechumens preparing for Baptism, who had to memorise it and be able to recite it to the Bishop. It is the secret of happiness. It is very important to note here that the first part of the *Catechism of the Catholic Church* offers a comprehensive, profound, and authoritative presentation and explanation of the Creed. It is a duty for adult Christians not only to read it but also to meditate on and study it because it contains immense riches.

87- What are the articles of the Creed?

This is our faith; this is the faith of the Church:
"I believe in one God, the Father Almighty, Maker of heaven and earth, of all things visible and invisible.
I believe in one Lord Jesus Christ, the only begotten Son of God, born of the Father before all ages, God from God, Light from Light, true God from true God, begotten, not made, consubstantial with the Father; through Him all things were made. For us men and for our salvation, He came down from heaven, and by the Holy Spirit was incarnate of the Virgin Mary and became man. For our sake He was crucified under Pontius Pilate, He suffered death and was buried, and rose again on the third day in accordance with the Scriptures. He ascended into heaven and is seated at the right hand of the Father. He will come again in glory to judge the living and the dead, and His kingdom will have no end.
I believe in the Holy Spirit, the Lord, the giver of life, who proceeds from the Father and the Son, who with the Father and the Son is adored and glorified, who has spoken through the prophets. I believe in one, holy, Catholic, and apostolic Church. I confess one baptism for the forgiveness of sins. I look forward to the resurrection of the dead and the life of the world to come. Amen."

88- What is the relationship between the Creed and our spiritual life?

There is a profound relationship between the Creed and our spiritual life. From the early centuries of the Church's life, it was not only considered the jewel of our life and faith but was also seen as the most beautiful prayer of the Christian. Saints like Athanasius and Basil the Great emphasised that the Creed could be said/sung like a Psalm, that is, "as a prayer."
The Creed is the reflection of our inner life or the "X-ray" of the Life within us; when we say or sing it, we are actually recounting what is happening deep within our hearts. "Proclaiming it" is

living a very intense moment where it seems that the veil covering the heart is lifted and allows us to see what is happening inside and what we hope to see more clearly. In fact, St. Teresa of Avila, reaching Union with the Lord Jesus (in the Seventh Mansion), says that what is believed in the other Mansions (before reaching Union), in that Mansion is *seen* (see *Interior Castle*, 7M 1,6). Thus, the Creed reminds us of the great truth of the Gospel that we must live from this earthly life in communion with the Trinity within our hearts (see *John* 14:23).

We ask Mary to teach us to live the Creed and to share her joy in praying it.

V- Walking the Extra Mile

89- Is it necessary to surpass ourselves?

The Lord invites us in the Gospel to make an effort to surpass ourselves. He also insists that without this effort, one does not "enter" into the Kingdom: "*For I tell you, unless your righteousness exceeds that of the scribes and Pharisees, you will never enter the kingdom of heaven*" (*Matthew* 5:20). We already know that the Pharisees and scribes were people quite committed to their faith. Proper charity begins with oneself, and if the Lord asks us to make an effort for others, He asks even more of us: "*If anyone forces you to go one mile, go with them two miles*" (*Matthew* 5:41). Our faith is called to grow, as we have said several times, but its growth depends on us, just as a plant cannot grow without sun and water. Every effort on our part to nourish our faith allows it to surpass its previous height. It is our responsibility to care for our faith, and no one will do it for us.

90- How to delve deeper into our faith?

The central element of our faith is our personal relationship with the risen Lord Jesus present in our lives. He calls us every day; we must listen to His voice, His call, and therefore take time and avoid distractions, and if necessary, empty ourselves of countless occupations.

The saints and masters of spiritual life have shown us how to do this and what to do to nourish our personal relationship with the Lord until discovering absolutely new and unheard-of depths.

One of the most effective practices for the growth of spiritual life is to meditate each week on the Passion of the Lord. Therefore, each week, one can take one of the Gospels and follow the Lord step by step in His Passion. Let us remember that every week of the year can resemble "Holy Week" in the sense that each week is a climb from the lowest (Monday) of where we find ourselves up to the highest of the Resurrection of the Lord (Sunday), passing through His Passion, sufferings, Death, and descent into Hell (Thursday, Friday, Saturday). Thus, each week becomes a moment of growth: struggle and victory in Christ.

The history of our faith is the story of people called to receive and experience the Love of God, and to receive it, we must make an effort to sit down, look at the Lord face to face, and let ourselves be loved by the Lord, heart to heart.

In this book, we have offered several points to ignite our faith and then nurture it every day; it is important to meditate on them and begin to put them into practice with perseverance.

In the following questions, we will explore some aspects of the Gospel to realise how many riches it contains and invite the reader to explore more.

91- What is the Transfiguration? and What is its role in our faith?

The Eastern tradition of the Church considers the Transfiguration of the Lord on Mount Tabor as a fundamental event that summarises all Christian prayer. The richness of their perception of the Transfiguration complements ours. The Greek Fathers say that Christ was "transfigured" from the moment of the Incarnation, that is, the moment when the Divine Nature united with the Human Nature in the one Person of the Divine Word. They also say that the ascent of the Apostles to this high mountain is the sign of the whole path of purification of the faith of the Apostles, and that they have been "transfigured" and therefore have been able to see Christ as He really is.

Like the Mass, the Transfiguration has two key moments: the first when Jesus' face and garments change appearance and Moses and Elijah appear, and the second when the luminous Cloud covers everyone, and the voice of the Father is heard.

The first moment refers to the spiritual experience of each believer during the readings of the Mass: the Old Testament (Moses - Pentateuch, Elijah - Prophets) and the New Testament (Jesus): the "face" and "garments" of the Word of God are transfigured and speak to us.

The second moment refers to the Eucharist where heaven opens and we receive with the Power of the Holy Spirit the Body and Blood of Christ, and thus during Communion the "cloud" of God covers us and *"Jesus alone"* remains (*Luke* 9:36), *"everything in everyone"* (*Colossians* 3:11).

With these brief explanations, we realise the richness of the Transfiguration and its role in our faith.

92- What is Faith in St. John?

St. John constructs his Gospel and catechesis around the act of "believing." He sets the goal of his Gospel: to became capable of "believing that Christ is the Son of God" (*John* 20:30-31). It implies a complete purification of the act of believing, and thus being able with the new act of faith to reach the Divinity of Christ and then receive the divine Life within us (see *John* 20:30). With St. John, we realise two things: the first is that believing is a journey (as we will see later) and that believing, or rather, being able to believe, is a true "victory" (see 1 *John* 5:4) and can be compared to the "Union with Christ" taught by spiritual masters.

To reach the full capacity of "believing," St. John offers us six signs plus a major one, which are like stages of growth and purification of our faith. The six signs are: 1- the wedding at Cana (*John* 2:1-11), 2- the healing of the official's son (*John* 4:46-54), 3- the healing of the paralytic (*John* 5:1-18), 4- the multiplication of the loaves and walking on water (*John* 6:1-27), 5- the healing of the man born blind (*John* 9), 6- the resurrection of Lazarus (*John* 11), and the great sign is the Passion, Crucifixion, Death, and Resurrection of the Lord (*John* 18-20). Like true "*servants*" (*John* 2:5), we must "fill" these six "jars" (see *John* 2:7) in order to taste the "*Good Wine*" (*John* 2:10) that flows from Christ's side on the cross (*John* 19:34-35). Therefore, we need to stop at each sign to meditate, contemplate, and receive the Holy Spirit who purifies and transforms us a little more into Christ each time, until we "*become like Him*" and "*see Him as He is*" (see 1 *John* 3:2), being united to Him and receiving His Life.

93- What is the role of the Cross in our Faith?

First of all, when we speak of the Cross, we refer to the Lord Himself crucified and to the Salvation that He is fulfilling on the Cross. The Lord accomplishes all Salvation on the Cross, and for that reason, the Cross is something immense; it transcends time, reaching every human being at any moment in history. It is concentrated and expresses all the Love of God and all His Glory. On the Cross, the Lord overcomes evil by transforming it completely into a higher good. The Cross has this unique power and capacity to absorb all evil and to convert it into love and forgiveness. The Cross is the most powerful lever in the world; it is capable of lifting and changing any negative situation. For these reasons, it is fundamental to approach it, entrusting all our burdens and our entire being to it, as all the saints did. Experiencing the powerful strength of the Cross, fear disappears, and Hope arises as a fundamental attitude. Thus, from the very beginning, when facing a new day we feel the powerful support of the Cross, and without expecting success, we feel "victorious," because "He loved us" first.

It is very important not only to turn to the Cross, trusting in It and surrendering to the Love of Christ radiating from It, but also to seek to live in the "area of Golgotha" within reach of the Love of the Crucified. This attitude is the marrow of Faith and deeply consolidates it.

94- What does "blessed are those who have not seen and yet have believed" mean?

Before making the act of faith, we have two elements before us: one is "evident," and the other is more "hidden." For example: Peter and a Pharisee see Jesus; neither of them sees the Divinity of Christ. The "evident" element, that is, the "visible," is the humanity of Christ; the invisible element is His Divinity. To make the act of faith, we need to see (or imagine) the humanity of Christ. This "seeing" is legitimate and necessary. The act of faith makes us, with the help of the Holy Spirit, move from the "visible" to the "invisible." It will then be Peter's choice to believe, while others will not want to believe.

Sometimes we initially wish to see the Divinity of Christ in an evident way, without taking the path that leads to it: the act of faith. For this reason, the Lord said, *"blessed are those who have not seen and yet have believed"* (*John* 20:29).

95- What does it mean to witness the Divinity of Christ?

Is it not the case that St. Mark "ends" his Gospel by placing these words into the mouth of the Roman Centurion, a witness to what happened on the Cross: *"Truly this man was the Son of God"* (*Mark* 15:39)? Is it not also the case that St. John places in the mouth of the Apostle Thomas these words: *"My Lord and my God"* (*John* 20:28)? Let us remember that we cannot see Jesus *"as He is,"* that is, His Divinity, if we have not been transformed into Him until *"becoming like Him"* (1 *John* 3:2). This leads us deeper into the authentic meaning of this confession of faith that the evangelists wanted to place at the end of their Gospel and their Catechesis. The goal of Christian formation, the goal of the formation of faith, is to offer a path of transformation through various stages of growth and purification until reaching the "fullness of faith." This means that at the same time we are being transformed into Jesus, we are taking on the likeness to Him we have lost and we are

75

seeing Him as He really is.

As we see, the "fullness of faith" is to reach the Divinity of Christ and is also a vision that implies the transformation of our entire being.

96- What does it mean to "confess the Mercy of Christ"?

One of the fundamental aspects of our faith is to experience the Mercy of the Lord. The first task of the Holy Spirit in our hearts is to show us two things simultaneously: the Mercy of God and our sin. It is through the merciful eyes of God that we can see our sin. It is only by knowing that we are loved that we can endure the ugliness of our sin. Thus arises contrition, which is this deep feeling inspired by the Holy Spirit, of having wounded the Heart of God.

We are all invited to confess the Love of God and to celebrate His Mercy in the sacrament of Reconciliation. This sacrament is a great help to having an authentic faith. As St. John says (see 1 *John* 4:1-6), whoever is of God confesses the Incarnation, and this sacrament is one of the extensions of the Incarnation to this day among us. Every time we overcome the shame of speaking about our sins to a fellow human being, every time we recognise the Presence of the Lord in the Priest, we confess the Incarnation of the Lord, and it extends to us.

97- What should our attitude towards Truth be?

Jesus' testimony before His judge, Pilate, was: "*I am a King. For this I was born, and for this I have come into the world, to bear witness to the truth. Everyone who is of the truth listens to my voice*" (*John* 18:37). "Seeking the truth" and, once found, "putting it into practice," is the mission of humanity on earth. This attitude nourishes our faith. It is essential to "know the truth"; therefore, every human being must put all their strength and resources into "seeking the Truth and putting it into practice." Sometimes it is said that "the truth hurts," but we must love it with all our strength and courageously prefer it above all else; it is that strong love that liberates us: "*If you remain in my teaching, you are truly my disciples, and you will know the truth, and the truth will set you free*" (*John* 8:31-32). The Words of Christ are truth itself; we must test them to verify that they are true and bearers of Life. It is our daily work to seek the light of Christ through His words and to experience the divine power enclosed in them.

Sometimes, unfortunately, we do as Pilate did and say to Jesus: "*What is truth?*" (*John* 18:38). Ironically Pilate had before him Jesus, who is the Truth itself (see *John* 14:6) and who communicates to us "*the Spirit of Truth*" (*John* 14:17). However, instead of having the necessary humility to seek the truth, Pilate expressed himself sarcastically saying, "*What is truth?*"

With the intercession of Mary and with the help of the Holy Spirit, let us commit ourselves to the search for Truth; it alone will make us happy.

Conclusion

I- Commit to renewing your Faith

98- Whose responsibility is it to renew faith?

Definitely, it is our responsibility to renew our own faith. No one can make this effort in our place. Therefore, we must commit to renewing our faith, deepening it, and exploring its riches. This book proposes the fundamental lines of faith for every believer and opens up new and practical horizons for its renewal. We must read these questions several times and meditate on the answers in order to put them into practice.

Faith is the greatest and richest talent that the Lord entrusts to every human being. At the end of life, the Lord will demand an account. It does not matter what age we are when we decide to take responsibility for our faith; what matters is today, as we read these lines, listening in our hearts to the voice of God speaking to us and the Spirit of God inviting us to awaken this Talent, to *"rekindle the gift of God"* (2 *Timothy* 1:6).

99- What is the importance of faith in everyday life?

As we have seen, our faith needs to grow every day like a seed that needs to develop and grow until it becomes a great tree. Growth takes place every day. Every day we have a step to take, a bread to receive to nourish our faith, as we say in the Our Father every day: *"give us this day our daily bread."* May this request be a reality every day. For this reason, the Lord told us, *"Do not work for the food that perishes, but for the food that endures for eternal life"* (*John* 6:27) and also, *"seek first the Kingdom of God and His righteousness, and all these things will be given to you as well"* (*Matthew* 6:33). The Lord does not ask us to divide our efforts between two searches (that of God and "the rest"); on the contrary, He invites us to put all our energy into the pursuit of one thing: *"the Kingdom of God,"* and assures us that "the rest" we do not have to ask for or worry about; instead, it will be given to us "as well." This is purity of heart: to place the Lord above all and serve Him and Him alone.

II- God the Father, end of our Faith

100- Who is the origin and end of our Faith?

God the Father is the origin of our Faith: "*Every good gift and every perfect gift is from above, coming down from the Father of lights, with whom there is no variation or shadow due to change. Of his own will he brought us forth by the word of truth, that we should be a kind of first fruits of his creatures*" (*James* 1:17-18).

Before creation, God the Father thought of us: "*Blessed be the God and Father of our Lord Jesus Christ, who has blessed us in Christ with every spiritual blessing in the heavenly places, even as he chose us in him before the foundation of the world, that we should be holy and blameless before him. In love he predestined us for adoption to himself as sons through Jesus Christ, according to the purpose of his will, to the praise of his glorious grace, with which he has blessed us in the Beloved*" (*Ephesians* 1:3-6).

Faced with such goodness, we can only say: "*Oh, the depth of the riches and wisdom and knowledge of God! How unsearchable are his judgments and how inscrutable his ways! 'For who has known the mind of the Lord, or who has been his counsellor?' 'Or who has given a gift to him that he might be repaid?' For from him and through him and to him are all things. To him be glory forever. Amen.*" (*Romans* 11:33-36).

God the Father is the end of our Faith: everything is done in the Son by the Holy Spirit to the Father.

"Glory to the Father and to the Son and to the Holy Spirit, as it was in the beginning, is now, and ever shall be world without end.
Amen."

Printed in Great Britain
by Amazon